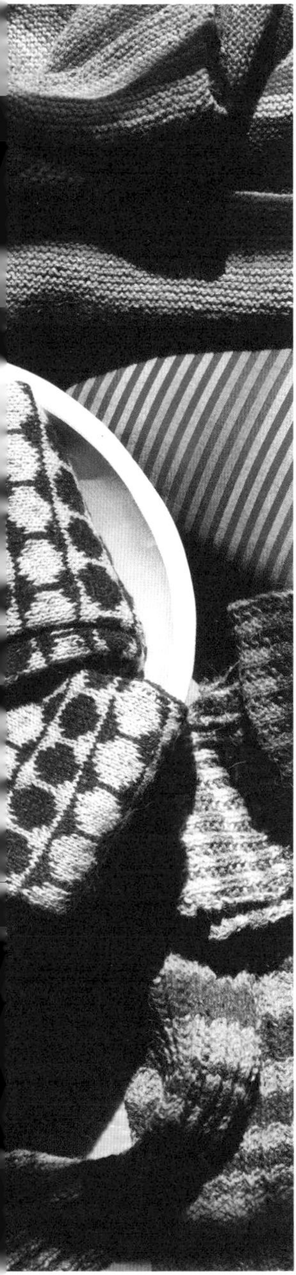

MDK FIEL

Master Class

Kay Gardiner and Ann Shayne

INTRODUCTION

WELCOME, DEAR KNITTERS, to a dream come true. In this Field Guide, we share with you the work of a person who is an unending source of inspiration and delight: Kaffe Fassett.

Some facts for those just getting to know Kaffe (whose name rhymes with "safe"). Although Kaffe has lived most of his life in England, he was born in California and grew up in one of the most dramatic natural places on Earth, Big Sur.

As a young painter with wanderlust, Kaffe headed to Britain in the 1960s. There, a chance meeting with Stephen Sheard, who was about to start a yarn company called Rowan, led Kaffe to a) learn to knit from a woman on a train and b) start designing knitting patterns. Kaffe used color with abandon, in a way that knitters had never done before. Using simple stripes, small stranded motifs, or bold graphic shapes, he ignored mundane concerns such as how many ends there would be to weave in. Then and now, Kaffe's work is iconoclastic, instantly identifiable, unforgettable.

Kaffe's credo: open your eyes and look around—color is everywhere. Instinct is a good designer. Don't worry about what goes with what. Keep putting colors next to each other to please your eye. Each color you add changes the composition of the whole. Never dither. Keep going. Finish the thing. Make the next thing. It's very simple. And it's full of joy.

How to Use This Field Guide

Think of this Field Guide as a master class with Kaffe, a chance to play and learn, have fun, and surprise yourself. Although some of the designs may look complicated to you at first glance, they are all based on the basic stripe, either solid or stranded. And they all use the same yarn—our beloved Rowan Felted Tweed. Once you figure out your gauge and needle size, you're set for multiple projects, and you will even have yarn left over from one project that you can then put to use in another.

There are two paths to take. You can follow Kaffe's stunning patterns for cushions, scarves, cowl, shawl, and throw as shown. Knitting them will be an elevating knitting experience. Watching Kaffe's colors build and interact will be glorious.

Or you can look at this Field Guide as a dictionary of stripes, to combine in solid or stranded sequences in whatever combinations and colors you like. It's your turn. Sit down with a pile of Rowan Felted Tweed and take off on your own adventure.

Just the way Kaffe does.

Kay Ann

STRIPED CUSHIONS

Design by

Kaffe Fassett

A PILE OF COLORFUL CUSHIONS has always been on our dream list of knitted projects, and with the ideas Kaffe provides, the possibilities are endless.

Start with a square or a rectangle. Think of these as extended swatches, the empty canvas that you can fill with as much color as you can fit in there.

The designs here include a cushion knit in the round, with a steek to cut. We love cutting a steek, so this is a good first project if you've never experienced the thrill of cutting into your knitting.

And if the idea of finishing a cushion seems daunting, we recommend buying a sofa cushion you like, knitting your square to fit the front, then whipstitching your finished square to the cushion. Done!

KNITTED MEASUREMENTS

12×12 (14×14, 16×16, 18×18, 20×20) (18×12, 20×12, 18×14, 20×14)" [30.5×30.5 (35.5×35.5, 40.5×40.5, 45.5×45.5, 51×51) (45.5×30.5, 51×30.5, 45.5×35.5, 51×35.5) cm]

MATERIALS

- Felted Tweed by Rowan [50 g skeins, each approx 191 yds (175 m), 50% wool/25% viscose/25% alpaca]: see quantities at right
- Size US 5 (3.75 mm) needles, or size needed to achieve gauge
- Cushion form 12×12 (14×14, 16×16, 18×18, 20×20) (18×12, 20×12, 18×14, 20×14)" [30.5×30.5 (35.5×35.5, 40.5×40.5, 45.5×45.5, 51×51) (45.5×30.5, 41×30.5, 45.5×35.5, 51×35.5) cm]
  Note: Change cushion form size as desired for fit or to customize striping.
- Matching sewing needle and thread (optional; for use with fabric back or steeking only)

GAUGE

24 sts and 32 rows = 4" (10 cm) over stockinette stitch, after blocking
24 sts and 33 rows = 4" (10 cm) over stranded stockinette stitch, after blocking. *Note:* Stranded row gauge varies from knitter to knitter. It is not essential to match row gauge exactly.

NOTES

Work cushion in stripes (see page 32) or stranded pattern (see page 38). When a stripe is complete, if you will use the same color again within next 10 rows, carry color up outside edge, twisting colors at beginning of row. Otherwise, cut yarn and weave in ends (or leave loose if you worked a steek).

See cushion back options on page 10.

If working stranded cushion front, you may find it easier to work front in round, using a steek, rather than working back and forth in rows. To do this, cast on an additional 5 steek stitches at end of round and join to work in round; the center of these 5 steek stitches will be cut after entire piece has been knit (see *Cutting the Steek*, page 11). Work the steek stitches in the colors used in the current round, alternating colors across the steek; work in one color if working a solid color round. Note that the 5 steek stitches are not included in stitch counts below.

YARN QUANTITIES

You'll need 1 ball each color for all Stripe Patterns and cushion sizes. If working solid knitted back, add 0 (1, 2, 2, 3) (1, 2, 2, 2) ball(s) color of choice. If mixing stranded patterns, you'll need approx 180 (240, 315, 395, 490) (265, 295, 310, 345) total yards. Divide total yardage by number of colors to determine yardage per color, adjusting for colors used more or less often.

Circus Stripes

Bright Colorway: 14×14" (35.5×35.5 cm) cushion (see page 33); Barbara, Electric Green, Scree, Turquoise, Mineral, Zinnia, Iris, Vaseline Green, Granite, Pink Bliss; fabric cushion back

Dusty Colorway: 12x12" (30.5x30.5 cm) cushion (see page 33); Seafarer, Granite, Tawny, Delft, Lotus Leaf, Peony, Seasalter, Amethyst, Avocado, Ginger. You will have enough Peony for back.

Ombré Stripes A

Bright Colorway: 18×12" (45.5×30.5 cm) cushion (see page 34); Scree, Granite, Clay, Vaseline Green, Turquoise, Pink Bliss, Barbara, Mineral, Zinnia, Maritime, and Iris; 1 ball Iris for cushion back

Ombré Stripes B

Dusty Colorway: 18×12" (45.5×30.5 cm) cushion (see page 35); Delft, Scree, Frozen, Peony, Avocado, Lotus Leaf, Amethyst, Seasalter, Ginger, Rage; 2 balls Lotus Leaf for cushion back

Caterpillar Stripes

Bright Colorway: 14×14" (35.5×35.5 cm) cushion (see page 32); Scree, Turquoise, Barbara, Vaseline Green, Mineral, Zinnia, Iris, Pink Bliss; fabric cushion back

Dusty Colorway: 12×12" (30.5×30.5 cm) cushion (see page 32); Peony, Scree, Lotus Leaf, Frozen, Ginger, Avocado, Seasalter, Camel; 1 ball Lotus Leaf for cushion back

Coins

Bright Colorway: 18×12" (45.5×30.5 cm) cushion (see page 40): Rage, Vaseline Green, Pink Bliss, Turquoise, Treacle, Avocado, Zinnia, Tawny, Seafarer, Stone, Mineral, Iris; 1 ball Vaseline Green for cushion back

Pinwheel

12×12" (30.5×30.5 cm) cushion (see page 48): Rage (A) and Avocado (B); 1 ball Avocado for cushion back

FRONT

- Using A, CO 72 (84, 96, 108, 120) (108, 120, 108, 120) sts.
- Beg chosen pattern; work even until piece measures approx 12 (14, 16, 18, 20) (12, 12, 14, 14)" [30.5 (35.5, 40.5, 45.5, 51) (30.5, 30.5, 35.5, 35.5) cm], ending with a WS row.
- BO all sts knitwise using color from last row worked.
- Weave in ends (or leave ends loose if you worked a steek). Block piece to measurements.

CUSHION BACK

To finish cushion, you have three options.

MATCHING KNITTED FRONT AND BACK

- Work back of cushion exactly the same as front.
- With RSs of front and back facing, carefully sew pieces together along 3 sides. Insert cushion form, then sew final side closed.

DIFFERENT KNITTED FRONT AND BACK

- Work back using a coordinating solid color or your choice of stripe or stranded pattern.
- With RSs of front and back facing, carefully sew pieces together along 3 sides. Insert cushion form, then sew final side closed.

FABRIC BACK

- Choose a coordinating fabric for back and work as follows:
- Cut fabric to 1" (2.5 cm) wider and longer than measurements of blocked front. This allows a ½" (1.5 cm) seam allowance along each edge. Fold each edge ½" (1.5 cm) to WS and press flat.
- With RSs of front and fabric back together, and using sewing needle and matching thread, carefully whipstitch 3 sides together. Turn piece RS out and insert cushion form, then whipstitch final side closed, making sure stitches do not show on RS.

CUTTING THE STEEK

The edges of the steek are secured as described below, and steek is cut, then finished with edging of choice.

Securing the Steek

Using sewing needle and a contrasting thread, sew one line along the center of stitch 2 of the steek from cast-on to bound-off edge, sewing across all color-change ends to anchor them. Be careful not to stretch or bunch up the knitted fabric as you sew, and not to catch the second layer of the piece. Begin and end the line with a few backstitches to anchor the edge. Turn and sew back along the same line, securing the beginning and end of the line. Repeat along the center of stitch 4. Using a pair of small, sharp scissors, cut along the center of stitch 3 of the steek. Continue cutting until you have reached the bound-off edge.

Your steeking is now complete, and you are ready to pick up for your preferred edging; pick up between the last steek stitch and the first stitch of the piece. When your edging is complete, fold the steeked edge to the wrong side and sew in place.

Pillows shown on following page (clockwise from top left): Bright Circus, Dusty Ombré, Bright Coins, Dusty Circus, Bright Caterpillar, Pinwheel, and Dusty Caterpillar.

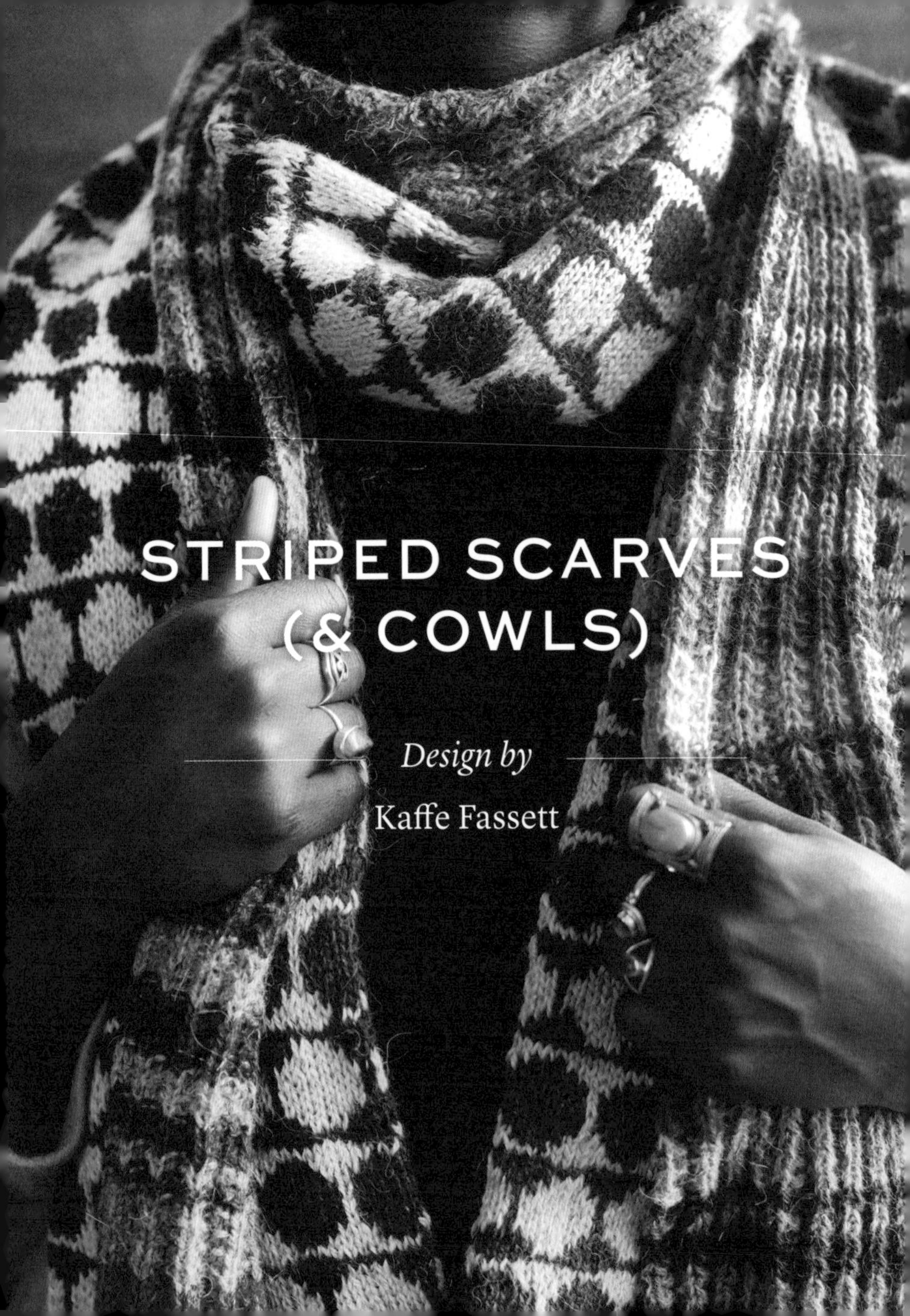

STRIPED SCARVES (& COWLS)

Design by

Kaffe Fassett

IN OUR EXCITEMENT about taking Kaffe's legendary stripes out for a spin, it's possible that we've gone the tiniest bit overboard. There are a lot of options here, and some of them are a substantial commitment of knitterly devotion.

But bear with us. Let's break down these stripey choices.

Tubular Striped Scarf

Do you like knitting 72-stitch tubes, around and around, until they get real long? This is the project for you! Choose any one of Kaffe's solid or patterned stripe patterns, grab your palette of Felted Tweed, and go. It's a long ride, but a fun one, with an epic accessory at the destination.

For the sample at left, we chose Kaffe's Coins in a grayed-out palette that proves what we always knew: gray is a color, and it's fascinating. For the two tubular scarves on page 18, we chose Checkerboard and Chevrons in both his Bright and Dusty colorways.

Mistake Rib Scarf

Is there a knitter who doesn't love mistake rib? For the sample on page 14, we chose Kaffe's Graduated Stripes in the Dusty colorway. The purls in this stitch pattern add little moments of texture that make it look quite different from the same stripe pattern in the crisp stockinette of the Tubular Striped Scarf.

Cowl

If you're looking to tiptoe into the waters of Kaffe, look no further. This Cowl allows you to play with any of Kaffe's stripes, solid or stranded, in a short 'n' snappy format. No muss—no fuss—great finished object. Valiant sample knitter Nell Ziroli had a blast knitting up the cowl in the Boxes and the Coins stranded stripe patterns (see page 39), but we can see many stunning, stylish possibilities: Checkerboard, Crosses, and even the wee Peerie pattern. These patterns pop, and they are totally modern.

KNITTED MEASUREMENTS

Mistake Rib Scarf: 5¾" wide × 80" long (14.5 × 203 cm); Tubular Scarf: 12" circumference × 80" long (30.5 × 203 cm); Cowl: 22¾" (58 cm) circumference × 11¼" (28.5 cm) height

MATERIALS

- Felted Tweed by Rowan [50 g skeins, each approx 191 yds (175 m), 50% wool/25% viscose/25% alpaca]: see page 52 for colors used in scarves and cowls shown in this Field Guide
- Mistake Rib Scarf: Size US 5 (3.75 mm) needles, or size needed to achieve gauge
- Tubular Scarf: Size US 5 (3.75 mm) double-point needles (set of 4 or 5), or size needed to achieve gauge
- Cowl: Size US 3 (3.25 mm) circular needle, 24" long; size US 5 (3.75 mm) circular needle, 24" long, or size needed to achieve gauge
- Stitch marker (Tubular Scarf and Cowl only)

GAUGE

Mistake Rib Scarf: 30 sts and 28 rows = 4" (10 cm) over Mistake Rib, after blocking

Tubular Scarf: 24 sts and 32 rows = 4" (10 cm) over stockinette stitch, after blocking

Stranded Scarf and Cowl: 24 sts and 33 rows = 4" (10 cm) over stranded stockinette stitch, after blocking

Note: It isn't essential to match row gauge exactly.

NOTES

You may work scarves in a stripe or stranded pattern (see pages 32–49).

When a stripe or motif is complete, if you will use the same color again within next 10 rows/rounds, carry color up outside edge/up WS, twisting colors at beginning of row/round. Otherwise, cut yarn and weave in ends.

If working a stripe pattern in the round, you may use Jogless Stripes (see page 19) for stripes of 2 or more rounds.

STITCH PATTERN

Flat Mistake Rib (multiple of 4 sts + 3)

- *All Rows:* K2, *p2, k2; repeat from * to last st, p1.

Circular Mistake Rib (multiple of 4 sts)

- *Rnd 1:* K1, p2, *k2, p2; rep from * to last st, k1.
- *Rnd 2:* *K2, p2; rep from * to end.
- Rep Rnds 1 and 2 for Circular Mistake Rib.

MISTAKE RIB SCARF

- Using A, CO 35 sts.
- Beg Mistake Rib and chosen stripe pattern; work even until piece measures approx 80" (203 cm), or to desired length, ending with a WS row, and ending at a visually pleasing point in the stripe pattern if you can't complete the stripe pattern.
- BO all sts in pattern using color from last row worked.
- Weave in ends; block as desired.

TUBULAR SCARF

- Using A, CO 72 sts. Join, being careful not to twist sts; pm for beg of rnd and work in the rnd as follows:
- Beg st st (knit every rnd) and chosen stripe or stranded pattern; work even until piece measures approx 80" (203 cm), or to desired length, ending at a visually pleasing point in the stripe or stranded pattern if you can't complete the pattern.
- BO all sts knitwise using color from last rnd worked.
- Weave in ends; block as desired. Sew CO edge closed; sew BO edge closed.

COWL

— Using smaller circular needle and color of choice, CO 136 sts. Join, being careful not to twist sts; pm for beg of rnd; work in the rnd as follows:
— Beg Circular Mistake Rib; work even until piece measures approx 1¼" (3 cm), working in one color or changing colors every 2 rounds, ending with Rnd 2 of pattern.
— Change to a larger circular needle and chosen stripe or stranded pattern; work even until piece measures approx 10" (25.5 cm), or to 1¼" (3 cm) less than desired length, ending at a visually pleasing point in the stripe or stranded pattern if you can't complete the pattern.
— Change to smaller circular needle and Circular Mistake Rib; work even, working ribbing in a solid color or working the stripes as at the beg of the cowl, until ribbing measures approx 1¼" (3 cm).
— BO all sts in pattern using color from last rnd worked.
— Weave in ends; block as desired.

JOGLESS STRIPES

Knitting stripes in the round means there's a spot where one round ends and the next begins. When colors change, this jump—or jog—is noticeable.

— To avoid a noticeable jog, when it's time to change colors, knit first stitch of the new color as you usually would. Knit the rest of the stitches to end of the round.
— On the next round, slip first stitch of new color, then knit the rest of the stitches.
— On every following round, knit every stitch as usual. The slip stitch tidies up the jog: a clever optical illusion.

Left: Tubular scarves in Checkerboard and Chevrons pattern (see page 42).

GARTER STRIPE SHAWL

Design by

Kaffe Fassett

THIS GENEROUS SHAWL uses our favorite, the humble garter stitch, in wide stripes that go on and on, with a subtle structure and order. This might be the largest project in this book, but it's also the easiest, and the most playful.

We're seeing this shawl doubling as a throw. It's the perfect project to keep by the sofa with a basket of Felted Tweed, working on it when we crave pure comfort knitting, and snuggling under it as soon as it gets to snuggable proportions.

KNITTED MEASUREMENTS

42" wide × 71" long (106.5 × 180.5 cm)

MATERIALS

- Felted Tweed by Rowan [50 g skeins, each approx 191 yds (175 m), 50% wool/25% viscose/25% alpaca]: 3 balls each Turquoise, Vaseline Green, Treacle, Iris, and Cinnamon; 2 balls each Zinnia, Pink Bliss, Mineral, Barbara, Celadon, and Electric Green; 1 ball each Scree, Clay, and Lotus Leaf
- Size US 5 (3.75 mm) circular needle, 40" (100 cm) long, or size needed to achieve gauge

GAUGE

24 sts and 44 rows (22 ridges) = 4" (10 cm) over garter stitch (knit every row), after blocking

NOTES

Working 2 rows in garter stitch creates 1 ridge.

It's a good idea to weave in ends as you go.

SHAWL

- Using Turquoise, CO 252 sts.
- Begin garter st (knit every row); work as follows:
  4 ridges (8 rows) in Turquoise,
  3 ridges (6 rows) in Treacle,
  6 ridges in Zinnia,
  4 ridges in Pink Bliss,
  2 ridges in Mineral,
  5 ridges in Vaseline Green,
  2 ridges in Scree,
  2 ridges in Clay,
  4 ridges in Treacle,
  6 ridges in Iris,
  8 ridges in Barbara,
  5 ridges in Pink Bliss,
  3 ridges in Clay,
  4 ridges in Lotus Leaf,
  6 ridges in Mineral,
  4 ridges in Celadon,
  5 ridges in Electric Green,
  13 ridges in Turquoise,
  6 ridges in Zinnia,
  4 ridges in Barbara,
  3 ridges in Pink Bliss,
  2 ridges in Scree,
  3 ridges in Clay,
  3 ridges in Vaseline Green,
  5 ridges in Cinnamon,
  8 ridges in Treacle,
  11 ridges in Iris,
  5 ridges in Barbara,
  8 ridges in Electric Green,
  5 ridges in Celadon,
  4 ridges in Zinnia,
  3 ridges in Mineral,
  7 ridges in Treacle,
  9 ridges in Cinnamon,
  3 ridges in Pink Bliss,
  3 ridges in Iris,
  5 ridges in Turquoise,
  3 ridges in Cinnamon,
  4 ridges in Celadon,
  2 ridges in Vaseline Green,
  3 ridges in Iris,
  1 ridge in Mineral.
- You are at the center of the Shawl. Now work the Stripe Pattern backwards, working 3 ridges in Iris, 2 ridges in Vaseline Green, 4 ridges in Celadon, etc. until you have worked back to the beg of the Stripe Pattern, ending with 4 ridges in Turquoise.
- BO all sts knitwise using Turquoise.
- Weave in rem ends; block as desired.

STRANDED STRIPE THROW

Design by

Kaffe Fassett

A JOLLY WEEKEND KNIT. Just kidding! The unabashed exuberance of this epic project celebrates so many of the things we love about Kaffe. For starters, his all-in approach: 24 motifs, from simple geometry to curvy vases, and 17 colors. No problem.

The temptation to follow Kaffe's choices is strong, but Kaffe would want us to go for it: lay out all the skeins, hang out with them a bit, then get going, reaching for whatever color looks good next to the one we just knit.

The finished size is actually on the small side for a throw—32¼ inches wide by 40½ inches tall. It's not much more knitting than a pullover. But it is such a delicious joy to work with so many colors, to make choices on whatever rounds we like, to see what happens when we combine unexpected pairs. It's very nearly foolproof to play in a project like this.

KNITTED MEASUREMENTS

32¼" wide × 40½" long (82 × 103 cm)

MATERIALS

- Felted Tweed by Rowan [50 g skeins, each approx 191 yds (175 m), 50% wool/25% viscose/25% alpaca]: 3 balls Frozen; 2 balls Peony; 1 ball each Lotus Leaf, Maritime, Pink Bliss, Amethyst, Pine, Treacle, Zinnia, Mineral, Iris, Vaseline Green, Avocado, Clay, Barbara, Rage, and Turquoise
- Size US 5 (3.75 mm) circular needles, 24" (60 cm) and 32" (80 cm) long, or size needed to achieve gauge
- Stitch marker

GAUGE

24 sts and 33 rows = 4" (10 cm) over stranded stockinette stitch, after blocking

Note: Stranded row gauge varies from knitter to knitter. It is not essential to match the row gauge exactly; however, if your row gauge differs, the length of the piece may not match the length given above. Adjust the length if you like by working additional motifs at the end.

SPECIAL TECHNIQUES

The last 5 stitches of the round will create a steek that will be cut after the entire piece has been knit (see *Cutting the Steek*, page 11). Work the steek stitches in the colors used in the current round, alternating colors across the steek; work in one color if working a solid color round. Note that the 5 steek stitches are not included in stitch counts below.

NOTES

When working stranded knitting, wherever possible, do not carry floats more than 6 stitches without trapping them. To trap a float, lay the non-working yarn over the working yarn, then work the next stitch with the working yarn. To preserve drape, do not trap floats more often than necessary.

If color will be used again within the next 10 rounds, carry color loosely up the WS; otherwise, cut color.

THROW

- Using 24" (60 cm) circular needle and Treacle, CO 174 sts. Join, being careful not to twist sts; pm for beg of rnd and work in the rnd as follows:
- *Set-Up Rnd*: Work Rnd 1 of Pattern Sequence (see below) to last 5 sts, pm, work steek sts (see Special Techniques) to end.

PATTERN SEQUENCE

- Work entire piece in st st (knit every rnd). The following instructions indicate whether to work a solid color or a charted motif. If working from a chart, you will be given the colors that correspond to each of the colors included in the chart. All charts beg with first st of chart, unless otherwise indicated. You might not complete full repeat of chart at end of rnd. When working from charts, omit any st(s) shaded in gray at end of chart.
- *Rnds 1-6*: Work Right Triangles Chart. A: Treacle; B: Vaseline Green.
- *Rnd 7*: Amethyst.
- *Rnd 8:* Pink Bliss.
- *Rnds 9-47*: Work Bowl of Fruit Chart. A: Barbara; B: Clay; C: Turquoise; D: Pine; E: Lotus Leaf; F: Avocado; G: Vaseline; H: Mineral.
- *Rnd 48*: Pink Bliss.
- *Rnd 49*: Frozen.
- *Rnds 50-55*: Work Left Triangles Chart. A: Pine; B: Mineral.
- *Rnd 56*: Rage.
- *Rnd 57*: Zinnia.
- *Rnd 58 and 59*: Work Right Peerie Chart. A: Clay; B: Iris.
- *Rnd 60*: Avocado.
- *Rnd 61*: Pine.
- *Rnds 62-75*: Work Swirls Chart, beg with st #16 of Chart. A: Maritime; B: Treacle.
- *Rnd 76*: Zinnia.
- *Rnd 77*: Peony.
- *Rnds 78 and 79*: Work Left Peerie Chart. A: Turquoise; B: Mineral.
- *Rnd 80*: Peony.
- *Rnd 81*: Zinnia.
- *Rnds 82-105*: Work Pitcher Chart. A: Amethyst; B: Turquoise; C: Clay.
- *Rnd 106*: Maritime.
- *Rnd 107*: Barbara.
- *Rnds 108 and 109*: Work Right Peerie Chart. A: Vaseline Green; B: Pine.
- *Rnd 110*: Barbara.
- *Rnd 111*: Frozen.
- *Rnds 112-133*: Work Pinwheel Chart. A: Rage; B: Avocado.
- *Rnd 134*: Maritime.

- *Rnds 135–138*: Work Half Diamonds Chart. A: Iris; B: Pink Bliss.
- *Rnds 139–146*: Work Squares and Right Triangles Chart, beg with st #13 of Chart. A: Mineral; B: Treacle; C: Zinnia.
- *Rnds 147–150*: Work Half Diamonds Chart. A: Pink Bliss; B: Iris.
- *Rnd 151*: Vaseline Green.
- *Rnds 152–157*: Work Right Triangles Chart. A: Lotus Leaf; B: Frozen.
- *Rnd 158*: Vaseline Green.
- *Rnd 159*: Pine.
- *Rnds 160–198*: Work Bowl of Fruit Chart. A: Electric Green; B: Clay; C: Turquoise; D: Rage; E: Barbara; F: Pink Bliss; G and H: Frozen.
- *Rnd 199*: Vaseline Green.
- *Rnd 200*: Turquoise.
- *Rnds 201–206*: Work Left Triangles Chart. A: Pine; B: Lotus Leaf.
- *Rnd 207*: Rage.
- *Rnd 208*: Amethyst.
- *Rnds 209 and 210*: Work Left Peerie Chart. A: Mineral; B: Treacle.
- *Rnd 211*: Peony.
- *Rnd 212*: Rage.
- *Rnds 213–226*: Work Swirls Chart, beg with st #16 of Chart. A: Turquoise; B: Zinnia.
- *Rnd 227*: Avocado.
- *Rnd 228*: Rage.
- *Rnds 229 and 230*: Work Right Peerie Chart. A: Electric Green; Mineral.
- *Rnd 231*: Treacle.
- *Rnd 232*: Maritime.
- *Rnds 233–256*: Work Pitcher Chart. A: Iris; B: Rage; C: Frozen.
- *Rnd 257*: Maritime.
- *Rnd 258*: Barbara.
- *Rnds 259 and 260*: Work Left Peerie Chart. A: Mineral; B: Pine.
- *Rnd 261*: Pink Bliss.
- *Rnd 262*: Electric Green.
- *Rnds 263–284*: Work Pinwheel Chart. A: Turquoise; B: Vaseline Green.
- *Rnd 285*: Maritime.
- *Rnds 286–289*: Work Half Diamonds Chart. A: Zinnia; B: Mineral.
- *Rnds 290–297*: Work Squares and Left Triangles, beg with st #13 of Chart. A: Avocado; B: Pine; C: Rage.
- *Rnds 298–301*: Work Half Diamonds Chart. A: Mineral; B: Zinnia.
- *Rnd 302*: Pink Bliss.
- BO all sts knitwise using Pink Bliss.

FINISHING

Weave in rem ends, being careful not to weave ends across steek sts. Using your preferred steek method (see page 11), steek sides of throw. Block steeked piece to measurements.

Log Cabin Border

- With RS facing, using 32" (80 cm) circular needle and Frozen, and working along long side edge, 1 st in from steek sts, pick up and knit approx 2 sts in every 3 rows along edge.
- Work in garter st (knit every row) until piece measures 2" (5 cm) from pick-up row, ending with a WS row.
- BO all sts knitwise on RS.
- Repeat for opposite long edge, leaving the last st on the needle.
- Rotate piece one quarter turn to the right. With RS facing, using Frozen, pick up and knit 1 st in each garter ridge of previous border, 1 st in each st along CO or BO edge, then 1 st in each garter ridge of next border.
- Knit 1 row.
- Work in garter st, slipping the first st of every row purlwise wyib until piece measures 2" (5 cm) from pick-up row, ending with a WS row.
- BO all sts knitwise on RS.
- Repeat for opposite edge.

ROWAN
FELTED
TWEED

Kaffe has been working with Rowan since 1980 when he met Stephen Sheard, the company's founder, at a workshop, and Stephen asked Kaffe if he had any color ideas for a new chenille yarn. Of course he did! Kaffe has been designing projects and consulting on yarns and colorways for them ever since.

Among Kaffe's favorite Rowan yarns is Felted Tweed, so he was thrilled when the company invited him to add some colors to the line in 2018 and then again in 2019 (for new colors to be released in 2020—stay tuned). "I enjoy the range's texture and atmosphere," Kaffe explains. "Its quality and fineness show off the detail I crave in my knitting. It also has a seductive silkiness."

About the pleasure of choosing new colors, he adds, "I look at what is in the current collection and then think about what, for me, is missing, usually higher and happier colors than the neutral and muted ones some seem to favor. My choices are based on what I want for my own knitting."

SOLID STRIPE PATTERNS

All of the solid stripe patterns in this Field Guide can be worked on any of the projects featured.

For Ombré, Caterpillar, and Graduated Stripes, after the first time the stripe pattern is worked, the colors are changed and the pattern is worked again with the new colors. Each repeat of the stripe pattern with a specified set of colors is called a "Unit." Each unit uses the same color letters (A, B, C, etc.); the colors corresponding to those letters change for each unit and are presented below the stripe pattern.

CATERPILLAR STRIPES

Working in st st (knit 1 row, purl 1 row flat; knit every rnd in the rnd) or Flat or Circular Mistake Rib (see page 17), *[work 2 rows/rnds in A, then 2 rows/rnds in B] 3 times; rep from * for Caterpillar Stripes, changing Unit colors every 12 rows/rnds as follows:

Bright Colorway

- *Unit 1*: A: Scree; B: Turquoise.
- *Unit 2*: A: Barbara; B: Vaseline Green.
- *Unit 3*: A: Mineral; B: Zinnia.
- *Unit 4*: A: Iris; B: Pink Bliss.

Dusty Colorway

- *Unit 1*: A: Peony; B: Scree.
- *Unit 2*: A: Lotus Leaf; B: Frozen.
- *Unit 3*: A: Ginger; B: Avocado.
- *Unit 4*: A: Seasalter; B: Camel.

Caterpillar Bright

Caterpillar Dusty

Circus Bright

Circus Dusty

CIRCUS STRIPES

Working in st st, work 10 rows in each of the following colors:

Bright Colorway: Barbara, Electric Green, Scree, Turquoise, Mineral, Zinnia, Iris, Vaseline Green, Granite, Pink Bliss

Dusty Colorway: Seafarer, Granite, Tawny, Delft, Lotus Leaf, Peony, Seasalter, Amethyst, Avocado, Ginger

GRADUATED STRIPES

Working in st st (knit 1 row, purl 1 row flat; knit every rnd in the rnd) or Flat or Circular Mistake Rib (see page 17), *work 2 rows/rnds in A, 2 rows/rnds in B, 4 rows/rnds in A, 4 rows/rnds in B, 6 rows/rnds in A, 6 rows/rnds in B, 8 rows/rnds in A, then 8 rows/rnds in B; rep from * for Graduated Stripes.

Bright Colorway

— *Unit 1*: A: Zinnia; B: Mineral.
— *Unit 2*: A: Vaseline Green; B: Barbara.
— *Unit 3*: A: Scree; B: Iris.
— *Unit 4*: A: Pink Bliss; B: Lotus Leaf.
— *Unit 5*: A: Vaseline Green; B: Zinnia.
— *Unit 6*: A: Mineral; B: Barbara.
— *Unit 7*: A: Scree; B: Lotus Leaf

Dusty Colorway

— *Unit 1*: A: Ginger; B: Delft.
— *Unit 2*: A: Tawny; B: Avocado.
— *Unit 3*: A: Seafarer; B: Amethyst.
— *Unit 4*: A: Peony; Scree.
— *Unit 5*: A: Ginger; B: Avocado.
— *Unit 6*: A: Seafarer; B: Delft.
— *Unit 7*: A: Tawny; B: Peony.

Graduated Bright

Graduated Dusty

OMBRÉ STRIPES

Flat Ombré Pattern A

- *Row 1 (RS)*: With A, knit.
- *Row 2*: With A, knit.
- *Row 3*: With A, purl.
- *Row 4*: With A, knit.
- *Row 5*: With B, knit.
- *Row 6*: With C, purl.
- *Row 7*: With D, knit.
- *Row 8*: With E, purl.
- *Row 9*: With E, knit.
- *Rows 10 and 11*: Rep Rows 8 and 9.
- *Row 12*: With D, purl.
- *Row 13*: With C, knit.
- *Row 14*: With B, purl.
- Rep Rows 1–14 for Flat Ombré Pattern A.

Circular Ombré Pattern A

- *Rnd 1*: With A, knit.
- *Rnds 2–4*: With A, purl.
- *Rnd 5*: With B, knit.
- *Rnd 6*: With C, knit.
- *Rnd 7*: With D, knit.
- *Rnds 8–11*: With E, knit.
- *Rnd 12*: With D, knit.
- *Rnd 13*: With C, knit.
- *Rnd 14*: With B, knit.
- Rep Rnds 1–14 for Circular Ombré Pattern A.

Working in Flat or Circular Ombré Pattern A, change Unit colors every 14 rows/rnds as follows:

Bright Colorway:

- *Unit 1*: A: Scree; B: Granite; C: Clay; D: Vaseline Green; E: Turquoise.
- *Unit 2*: A: Scree; B: Granite; C: Clay; D: Pink Bliss; E: Barbara.
- *Unit 3*: A: Scree; B: Granite; C: Clay; D: Mineral; E: Zinnia.
- *Unit 4*: A: Scree; B: Granite; C: Clay; D: Maritime; E: Iris.
- To finish off piece, work Rows/Rnds 1–3 once more.

Flat Ombré Pattern B

- *Row 1 (RS)*: With A, knit.
- *Row 2*: With A, knit.
- *Row 3*: With A, purl.
- *Row 4*: With A, knit.
- *Row 5*: With B, knit.
- *Row 6*: With C, purl.
- *Row 7*: With D, knit.
- *Row 8*: With D, purl.
- *Rows 9 and 10*: Rep Rows 7 and 8.
- *Row 11*: With C, knit.
- *Row 12*: With B, purl.
- Rep Rows 1–12 for Flat Ombré Pattern B.

Circular Ombré Pattern B

- *Rnd 1*: With A, knit.
- *Rnds 2–4*: With A, purl.
- *Rnd 5*: With B, knit.
- *Rnd 6*: With C, knit.
- *Rnds 7–10*: With D, knit.
- *Rnd 11*: With C, knit.
- *Rnd 12*: With B, knit.
- Rep Rnds 1–12 for Circular Ombré Pattern B.

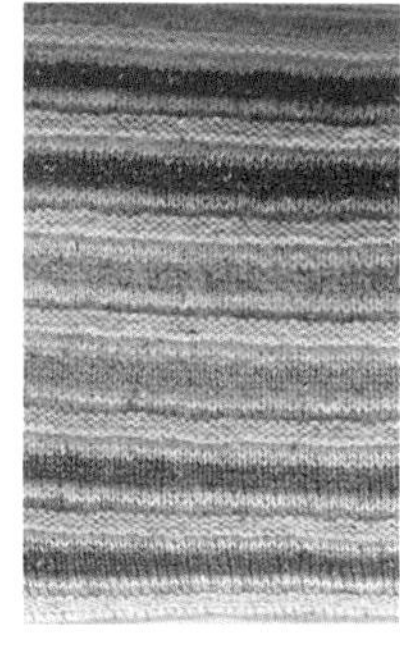

Ombré Bright

Ombré Dusty

Working in Flat or Circular Ombré Pattern B, change Unit colors every 12 rows/rnds as follows:

Dusty Colorway

- *Unit 1*: A: Delft; B: Scree; C: Frozen; D: Peony.
- *Unit 2*: A: Delft; B: Scree; C: Avocado; D: Lotus Leaf.
- *Unit 3*: A: Delft; B: Scree; C: Amethyst; D: Seasalter.
- *Unit 4*: A: Delft; B: Scree; C: Ginger; D: Rage.
- To finish off piece, work Rows/Rnds 1–3 once more.

STRANDED STRIPE PATTERNS

These stranded stripe patterns are all interchangeable.

Work these patterns in stockinette stitch (knit 1 row, purl 1 row flat; knit every round in the round).

When working stranded knitting, do not carry floats more than 6 stitches without trapping them. To trap a float, lay the non-working yarn over the working yarn, then work the next stitch with the working yarn. To preserve drape, do not trap floats more often than necessary. If a color will be used again within the next 10 rounds, carry the color loosely up the wrong side; otherwise cut the color.

The stranded patterns below are a combination of charted motifs and single-color rounds/rows. The colors may change from one instance of a particular motif to the next instance of the same motif further up the piece. The color(s) to be used for a round/row will always be given.

For the Coins Chart and Boxes Chart, after the first time the chart pattern is worked, the colors are changed and the pattern is worked again with the new colors. Each vertical repeat of the chart with a specified set of colors is called a "Unit". Each unit uses the same color letters (A, B, C, D); the colors corresponding to those letters change for each unit and are presented below the stranded pattern.

Depending on your project and the stranded pattern you are using, you might not complete an entire vertical pattern repeat before reaching the specified length. Be sure to finish the piece in a visually pleasing manner, even if it is not the end of the vertical pattern repeat.

You can also use these charts to create your own stranded projects. Insert solid-color rounds/rows and/or Peerie charts between larger charts so that the motifs stand alone.

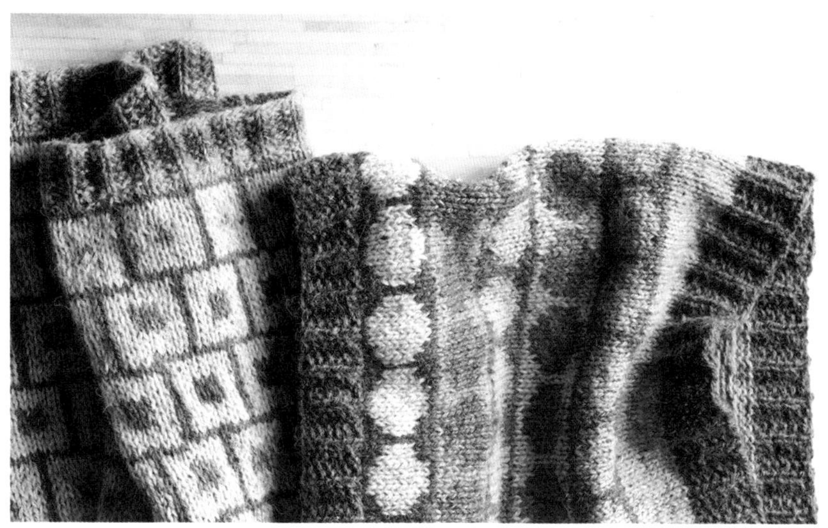

If you are working a circular project, work just the stitches shown for the pattern repeat, omitting the additional stitch(es) shaded in gray. If your project is intended to be a flat piece (for example a throw or cushion front or back), you may either work the piece flat or in the round using steeks (see *Cutting the Steek*, page 11); work the gray-shaded stitches, which are intended to balance the motif at both sides of the piece.

Since not all of the charts have the same stitch pattern repeat, you may wish to plan your design so the center of each chart is at the center of the round/row, and count out from the center to determine what stitch you should begin with. Each chart has the center marked on it. For charts with an even number of stitches, the center will be between two stitches; for odd, you will have a single center stitch.

BOXES

Working Rnds 1–20 of Boxes Chart, change Unit colors every 20 rnds as follows:

Dusty Colorway (see above)

- *Unit 1*: A: Amethyst; B: Alabaster; C: Vaseline Green; D: Avocado.
- *Unit 2*: A: Amethyst; B: Alabaster; C: Pink Bliss; D: Maritime.
- *Unit 3*: A: Amethyst; B: Alabaster; C: Vaseline Green; D: Frozen.
- *Unit 4*: A: Amethyst; B: Alabaster; C: Zinnia; D: Iris.
- Rep Units 1–4 for Dusty Colorway, then work Rnd 21 of chart once.

Boxes

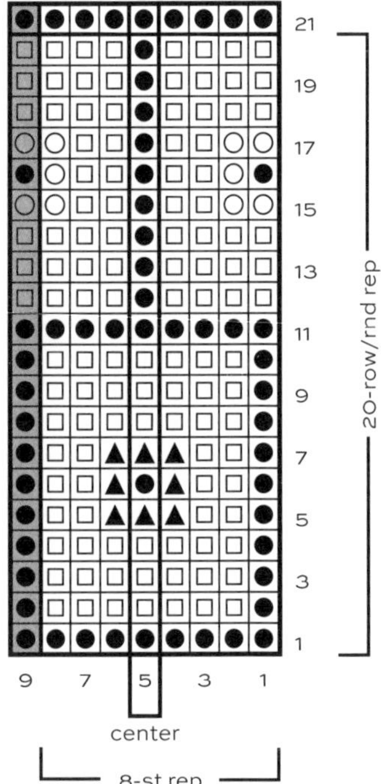

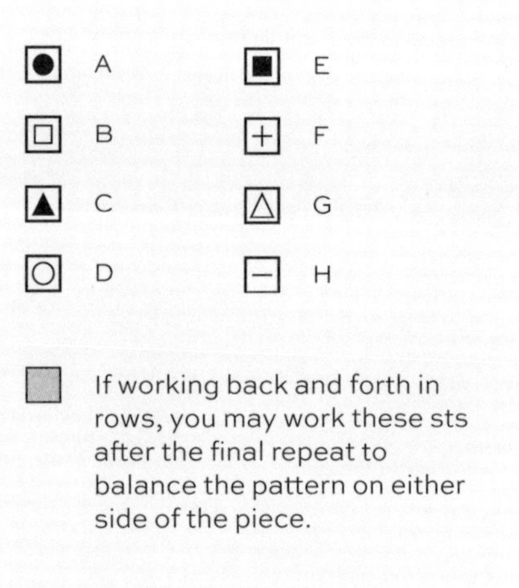

Bright Colorway (see page 40)

— *Unit 1*: A: Seafarer; B: Scree; C: Electric Green; D: Zinnia.
— *Unit 2*: A: Seafarer; B: Scree; C: Rage; D Lotus Leaf.
— *Unit 3*: A: Seafarer; B: Scree; C: Electric Green; D: Iris.
— *Unit 4*: A: Seafarer; B: Scree; C: Turquoise; D: Ginger.
— Rep Units 1–4 for Bright Colorway, then work Rnd 21 of chart once.

COINS

Working Rnds 1–20 of Coins Chart, change Unit colors every 20 rnds as follows:

Two-Color Colorway (see pages 5 & 39)

Unit 1: A and D: Seafarer; B and C: Clay.
— Rep Unit 1 for Two-Color Colorway.

Bright Colorway (see pages 5 & 39)

— *Unit 1*: A: Rage; B: Vaseline Green; C: Pink Bliss; D: Turquoise.
— *Unit 2*: A: Treacle; B: Avocado; C: Zinnia; D: Tawny.
— *Unit 3*: A: Seafarer; B: Stone; C: Mineral; D: Iris.
— *Unit 4*: A: Turquoise; B: Pink Bliss; C: Vaseline Green; D: Rage.

- *Unit 5*: A: Iris; B: Zinnia; C: Stone; D: Seafarer.
- *Unit 6*: A: Rage; B: Mineral; C: Avocado; D: Turquoise.
- *Unit 7*: A: Treacle; B: Pink Bliss; C: Zinnia; D: Seafarer.
- *Unit 8*: A: Seafarer; B: Stone; C: Mineral; D: Turquoise.
- Rep Units 1–8 for Bright Colorway.

Coins

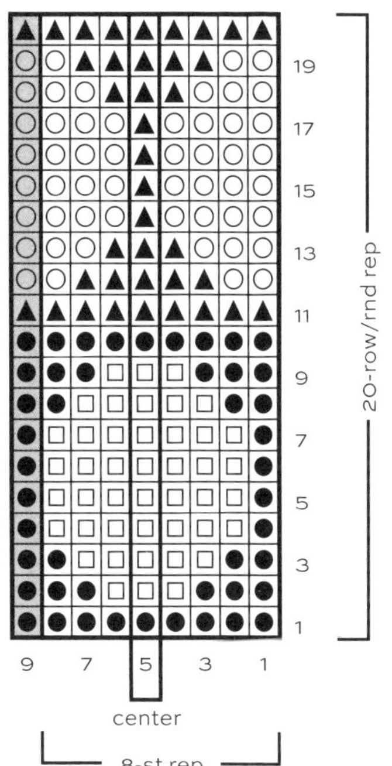

Dusty Colorway (see pages 5 & 39)

Unit 1: A: Peony; B: Alabaster; C: Mineral; D: Pink Bliss.

- *Unit 2*: A: Amethyst; B: Scree; C: Alabaster; D: Avocado.
- *Unit 3*: A: Pink Bliss; B: Frozen; C: Scree; D: Vaseline Green.
- *Unit 4*: A: Peony; B: Mineral; C: Frozen; D: Maritime.
- *Unit 5*: A: Avocado; B: Scree; C: Alabaster; D: Vaseline Green.
- *Unit 6*: A: Pink Bliss; B: Mineral; C: Scree; D: Amethyst.
- *Unit 7*: A: Maritime; B: Frozen; C: Alabaster; D: Pink Bliss.
- *Unit 8*: A: Avocado; B: Mineral; C: Frozen; D: Amethyst.
- Rep Units 1–8 for Dusty Colorway.

Right Chevron

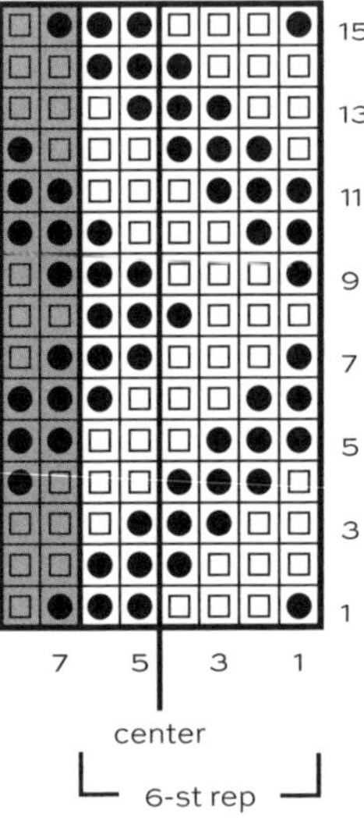

Left Chevron

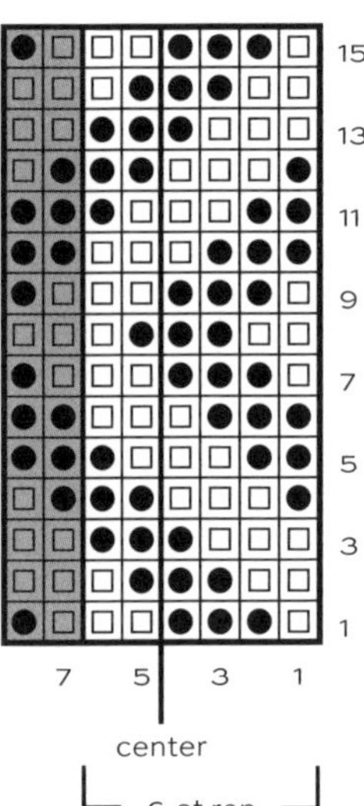

Checkerboard

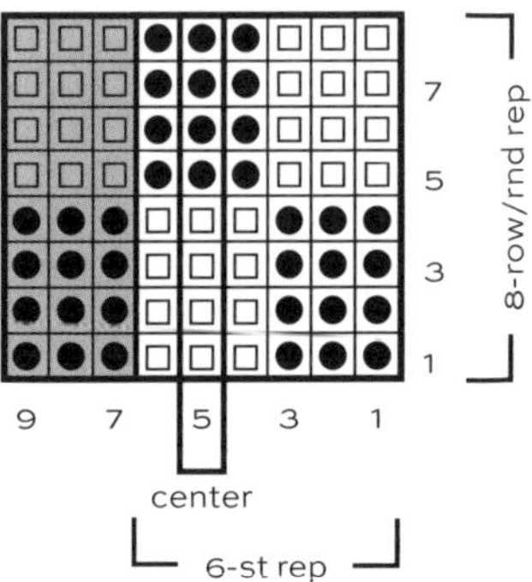

Left Peerie Right Peerie

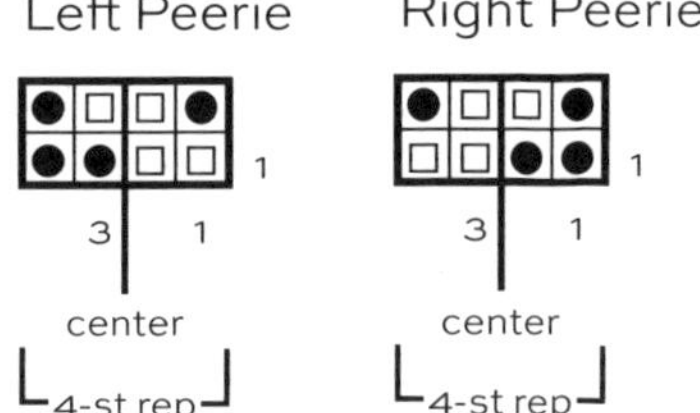

CHECKERBOARD AND CHEVRONS

Bright Colorway (see page 18)

- *Rnds 1–16*: Work Checkerboard Chart. A: Seafarer; B: Scree.
- *Rnd 17*: Rage.
- *Rnd 18 and 19*: Work Right Peerie Chart. A: Turquoise; B: Pink Bliss.
- *Rnd 20*: Rage.
- *Rnds 21–27*: Work Ring Chart. A: Lotus Leaf; B: Vaseline Green.
- *Rnd 28*: Rage.

Ring

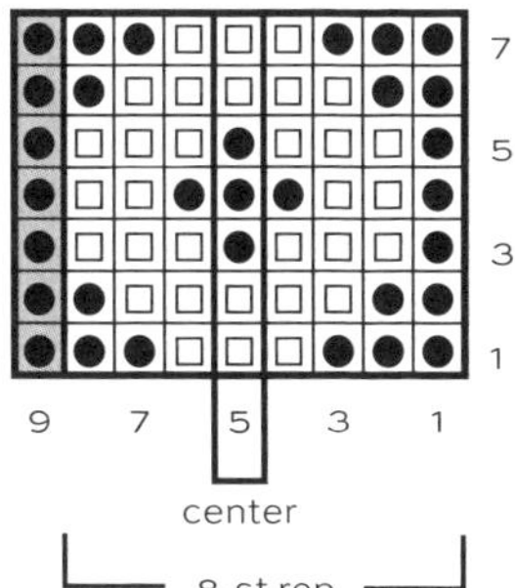

Diamond

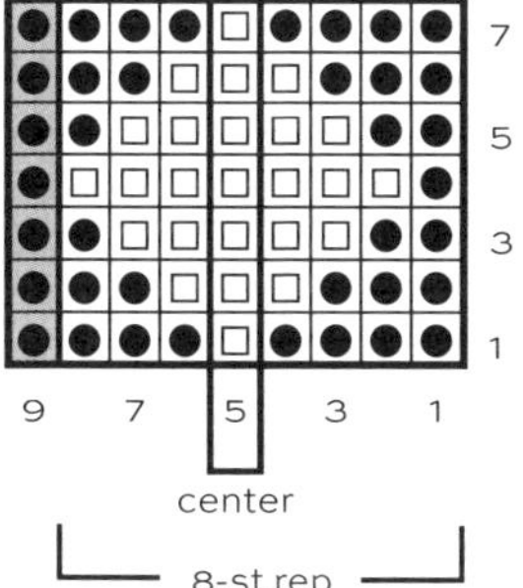

- *Rnds 29 and 30*: Work Left Peerie Chart. A: Turquoise; B: Pink Bliss.
- *Rnd 31*: Rage.
- *Rnds 32–46*: Work Right Chevron Chart. A: Seafarer; B: Scree.
- *Rnd 47*: Electric Green.
- *Rnds 48 and 49*: Work Right Peerie Chart. A: Rage; B: Mineral.
- *Rnd 50*: Electric Green.
- *Rnds 51–57*: Work Diamond Chart. A: Tawny; B: Zinnia.
- *Rnd 58*: Electric Green.

Star

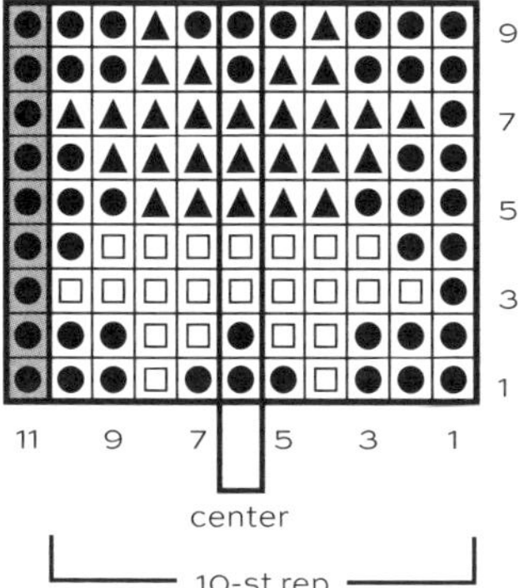

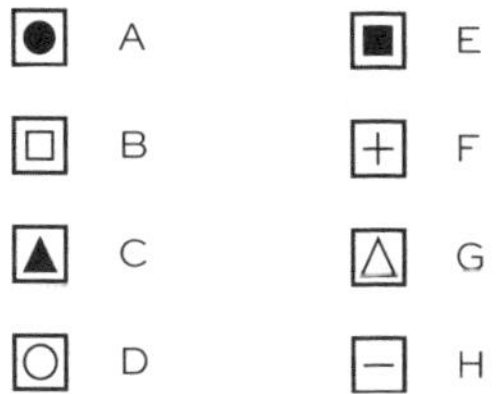

If working back and forth in rows, you may work these sts after the final repeat to balance the pattern on either side of the piece.

Right Crosses

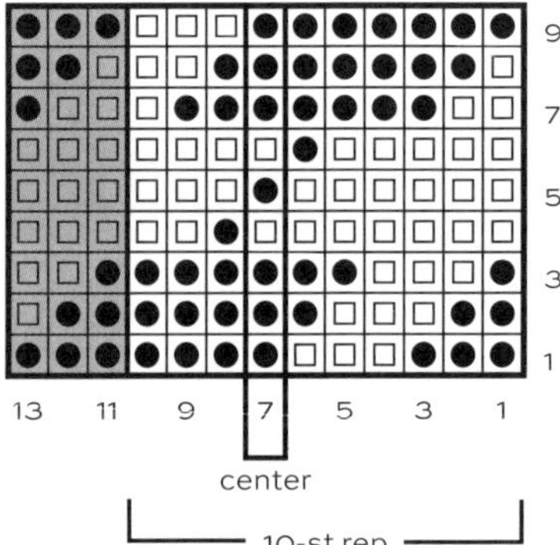

Left Crosses

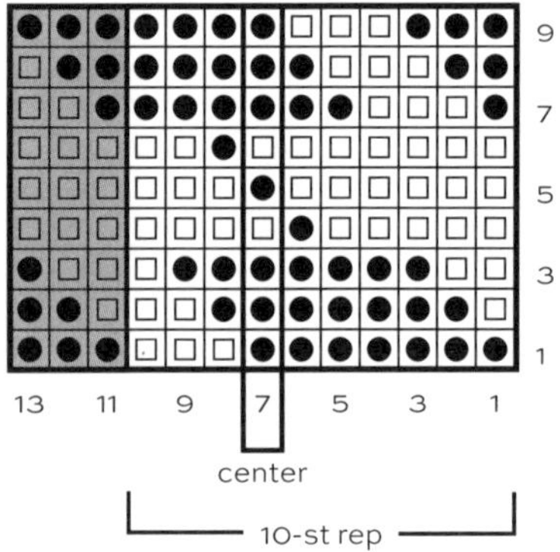

- *Rnds 59 and 60*: Work Left Peerie Chart. A: Rage; B: Mineral.
- *Rnd 61*: Electric Green.
- *Rnds 62–77*: Work Checkerboard Chart. A: Seafarer; B: Scree.
- *Rnd 78*: Pink Bliss.
- *Rnds 79 and 80*: Work Right Peerie Chart. A: Lotus Leaf; B: Frozen.
- *Rnd 81*: Pink Bliss.
- *Rnds 82–90*: K1 in A, work Left Crosses Chart to last st, k1 in A. A: Turquoise; B: Avocado.
- *Rnd 91*: Pink Bliss.
- *Rnds 92 and 93*: Work Left Peerie Chart. A: Lotus Leaf; B: Frozen.
- *Rnd 94*: Pink Bliss.
- *Rnds 95–109*: Work Left Chevron Chart. A: Seafarer; B: Scree.
- *Rnd 110*: Zinnia.
- *Rnds 111 and 112*: Work Right Peerie Chart. A: Amethyst; B: Mineral.
- *Rnds 113*: Zinnia.
- *Rnds 114–122*: K1 in A, work Star Chart to last st, k1 in A. A: Rage; B: Barbara; C: Pink Bliss.
- *Rnd 123*: Zinnia.
- *Rnds 124 and 125*: Work Left Peerie Chart. A: Amethyst; B: Mineral.
- *Rnds 126*: Zinnia.
- Rep Rnds 1–126 for Bright Colorway.

Dusty Colorway (see page 19)

- *Rnds 1–16*: Work Checkerboard Chart. A: Maritime; B: Alabaster.
- *Rnd 17*: Pink Bliss.

Symbol	Color	Symbol	Color
●	A	■	E
□	B	+	F
▲	C	△	G
○	D	–	H

(gray box) If working back and forth in rows, you may work these sts after the final repeat to balance the pattern on either side of the piece.

- *Rnd 18 and 19*: Work Right Peerie Chart. A: Peony; B: Camel.
- *Rnd 20*: Pink Bliss.
- *Rnds 21–27*: Work Ring Chart. A: Clay; B: Avocado.
- *Rnd 28*: Pink Bliss.
- *Rnd 29 and 30*: Work Left Peerie Chart. A: Peony; B: Camel.
- *Rnd 31*: Pink Bliss.
- *Rnds 32–46*: Work Left Chevron Chart. A: Maritime; B: Alabaster.
- *Rnd 47*: Mineral.
- *Rnds 48 and 49*: Work Right Peerie Chart. A: Amethyst; B: Frozen.
- *Rnd 50*: Mineral.
- *Rnds 51–57*: Work Diamond Chart. A: Clay; B: Pink Bliss.
- *Rnd 58*: Mineral.
- *Rnds 59 and 60*: Work Left Peerie Chart. A: Amethyst; B: Frozen.
- *Rnd 61*: Mineral.
- *Rnds 62–77*: Work Checkerboard Chart. A: Maritime; B: Alabaster.
- *Rnd 78*: Peony.
- *Rnds 79 and 80*: Work Right Peerie Chart. A: Iris; B: Frozen.
- *Rnd 81*: Peony.
- *Rnds 82–90*: K1 in A, work Right Crosses Chart to last st, k1 in A. A: Clay; B: Vaseline Green.
- *Rnd 91*: Peony.
- *Rnds 92 and 93*: Work Left Peerie Chart. A: Iris; B: Frozen.
- *Rnd 94*: Peony.
- *Rnds 95–109*: Work Right Chevron Chart. A: Maritime; B: Alabaster.
- *Rnd 110*: Avocado.
- *Rnds 111 and 112*: Work Right Peerie Chart. A: Amethyst; B: Frozen.
- *Rnds 113*: Avocado.
- *Rnds 114–122*: K1 in A, work Star Chart to last st, k1 in A. A: Clay; B and C: Peony.
- *Rnd 123*: Avocado.
- *Rnds 124 and 125*: Work Left Peerie Chart. A: Amethyst; B: Frozen.
- *Rnds 126*: Avocado.
- Rep Rnds 1–126 for Dusty Colorway.

Fruit

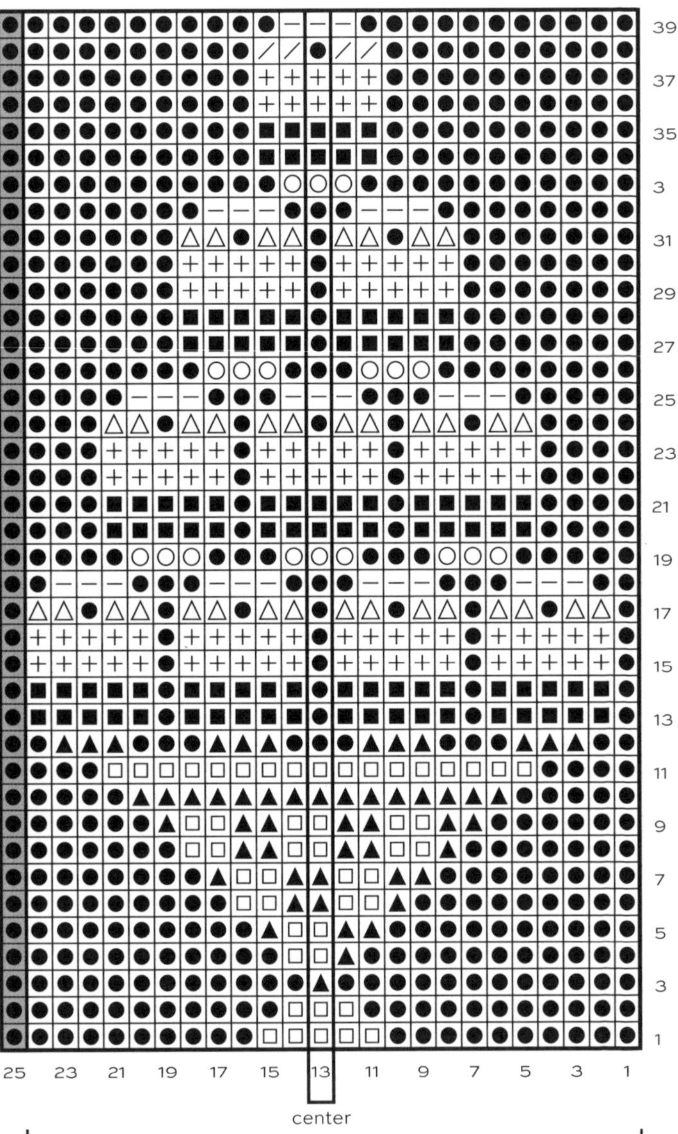
39
37
35
3
31
29
27
25
23
21
19
17
15
13
11
9
7
5
3
1
25
23
21
19
17
15
13
11
9
7
5
3
1
center
24-st rep

Pitcher

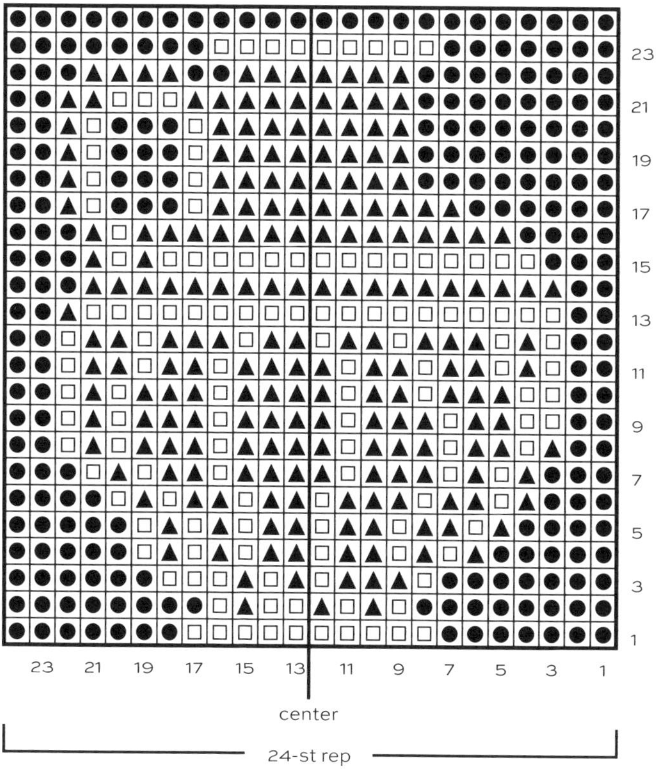

Row	24	23	22	21	20	19	18	17	16	15	14	13	12	11	10	9	8	7	6	5	4	3	2	1
24	A	A	A	A	A	A	A	A	A	A	A	A	A	A	A	A	A	A	A	A	A	A	A	A
23	A	A	A	A	A	A	A	A	B	B	B	B	B	B	B	B	B	A	A	A	A	A	A	A
22	A	A	A	C	C	C	C	A	A	C	C	C	C	C	C	C	A	A	A	A	A	A	A	A
21	A	A	C	C	B	B	B	C	C	C	C	C	C	C	C	C	A	A	A	A	A	A	A	A
20	A	A	C	B	A	A	A	B	C	C	C	C	C	C	C	C	A	A	A	A	A	A	A	A
19	A	A	C	B	A	A	A	B	C	C	C	C	C	C	C	C	A	A	A	A	A	A	A	A
18	A	A	C	B	A	A	A	B	C	C	C	C	C	C	C	C	A	A	A	A	A	A	A	A
17	A	A	C	B	A	A	A	B	C	C	C	C	C	C	C	C	C	C	A	A	A	A	A	A
16	A	A	A	C	B	C	C	C	C	C	C	C	C	C	C	C	C	C	C	C	A	A	A	A
15	A	A	A	C	B	C	B	B	B	B	B	B	B	B	B	B	B	B	B	B	B	A	A	A
14	A	A	A	C	C	C	C	C	C	C	C	C	C	C	C	C	C	C	C	C	C	C	A	A
13	A	A	C	B	B	B	B	B	B	B	B	B	B	B	B	B	B	B	B	B	B	B	A	A
12	A	A	B	C	C	B	C	C	C	B	C	C	B	C	C	B	C	C	C	B	C	B	A	A
11	A	A	B	C	C	B	C	C	B	C	C	C	C	B	C	C	B	C	C	B	C	B	A	A
10	A	A	B	C	B	C	C	C	B	C	C	C	C	B	C	C	B	C	C	C	B	B	A	A
9	A	A	B	C	B	C	C	C	B	C	C	C	C	B	C	C	C	B	C	C	B	B	A	A
8	A	A	B	C	B	C	C	C	B	C	C	C	C	B	C	C	C	B	C	C	B	C	A	A
7	A	A	A	B	C	B	C	C	B	C	C	C	C	B	C	C	C	B	C	B	C	A	A	A
6	A	A	A	A	B	C	B	C	C	B	C	C	B	C	C	C	B	C	C	B	C	A	A	A
5	A	A	A	A	A	B	C	B	C	B	C	C	B	C	C	B	C	C	B	C	A	A	A	A
4	A	A	A	A	A	B	C	B	C	B	C	C	B	C	C	B	C	B	C	A	A	A	A	A
3	A	A	A	A	A	A	B	B	B	C	B	C	B	C	C	C	B	A	A	A	A	A	A	A
2	A	A	A	A	A	A	A	A	B	C	B	B	C	B	C	B	A	A	A	A	A	A	A	A
1	A	A	A	A	A	A	A	B	B	B	B	B	B	B	B	B	B	A	A	A	A	A	A	A

center

24-st rep

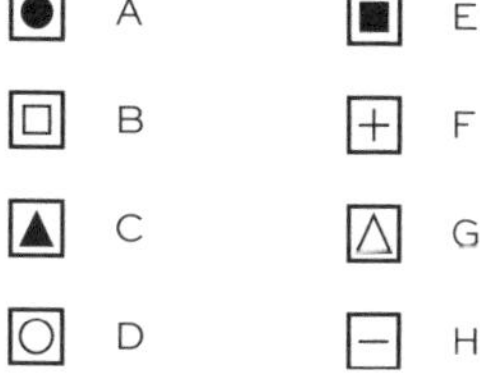

If working back and forth in rows, you may work these sts after the final repeat to balance the pattern on either side of the piece.

Pinwheel

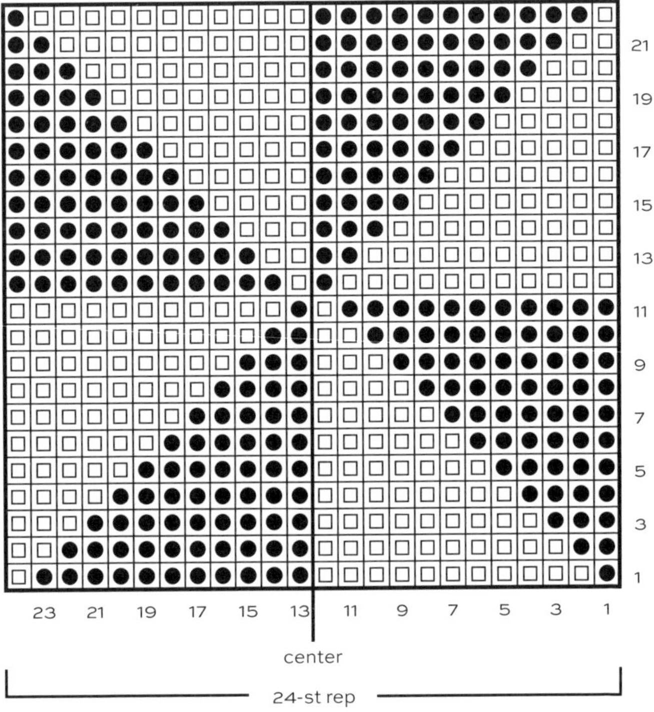

Half Diamonds

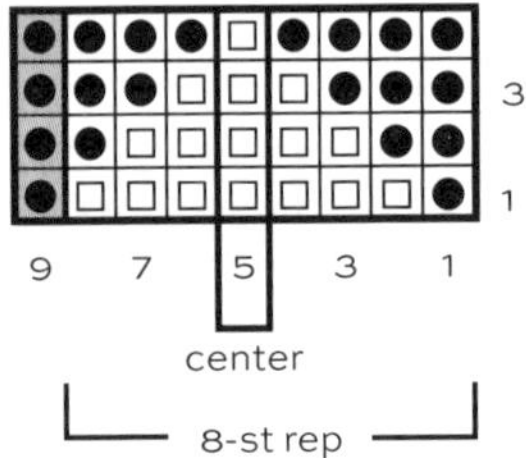

Squares and Left Triangles

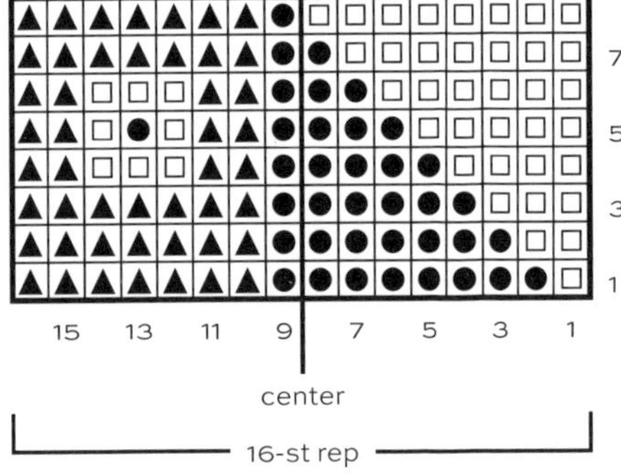

Squares and Right Triangles

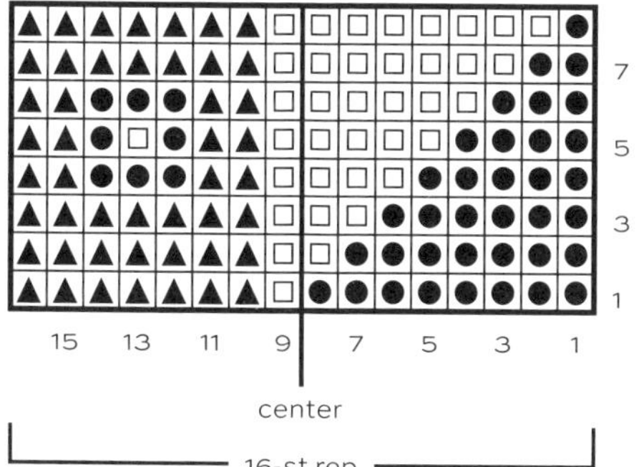

Swirls

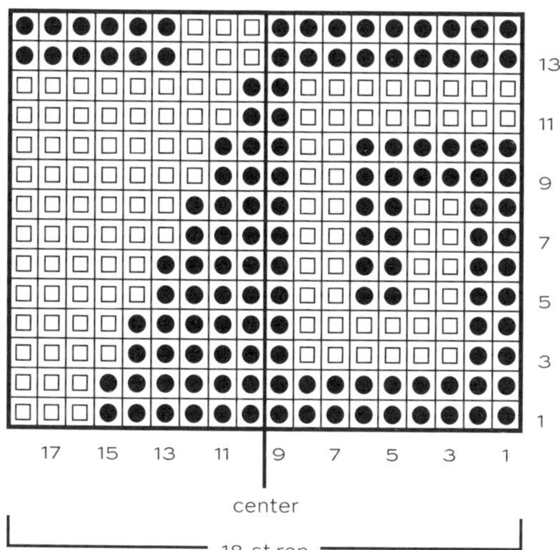

Left Triangles

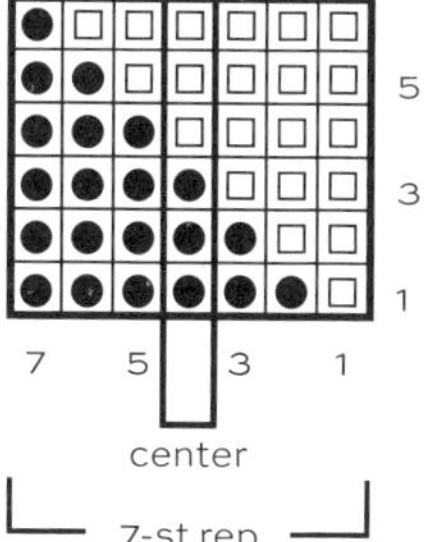

Right Triangles

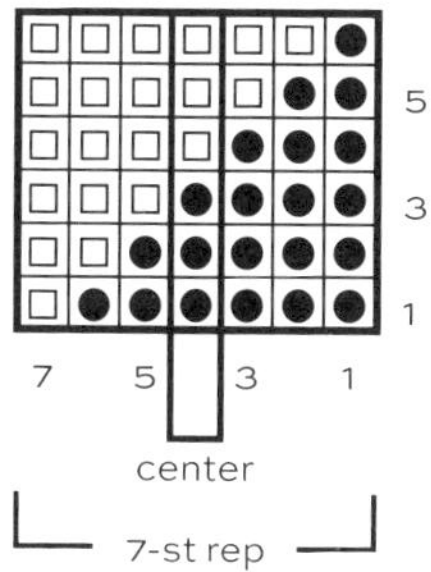

A

B

C

D

E

F

G

H

If working back and forth in rows, you may work these sts after the final repeat to balance the pattern on either side of the piece.

MEET KAFFE FASSETT

Spending time with Kaffe's kaleidoscopic work will lift your spirits—the unabashed joy of it all is what we love most about this extraordinary artist. He's game to explore color and pattern in all sorts of materials: knitwear, patchwork, needlepoint, painting, and mosaic. He is the author of many books, all stacked with ideas, and just when we think we've got the hang of Kaffe, he surprises us yet again. Begin your own exploration of the master with this Field Guide, his website, kaffefassett.com, and his autobiography, *Dreaming in Color*.

Wondering what it might feel like to walk in his shoes? We reached out with a few questions.

When you're at home in London, what does a typical day look like?
I get up around 7 am every morning and head to the studio with a cup of hot water. Brandon prepares breakfast —homemade granola and fruit salad— which we eat together at about 7:30. Then we go to work designing in the studio: knitting swatches for new projects, stitching needlepoint, or painting fabric prints for the next collection. I'm usually very focused on whatever I'm doing, but if I lose focus, I change to another project. And I take a power nap after lunch.

At 5:30 pm I walk a couple of miles to my gym, stopping off at Starbucks to have a soya chai latte and do the daily crossword puzzle in the *Evening Standard*. I spend about an hour on the treadmill and the rowing machine at the gym, then I go home to work in the studio until dinner is ready, then TV till 10 pm, then bed.

What do you like to do to relax?
At home I'll do simple handwork like needlepoint or stitching a binding onto a quilt while watching TV or listening to a play or a reading of a novel on BBC 4. When I'm traveling and teaching, I'll go to a museum to see what is happening in the local art scene. I'm always looking for more inspiration for patterns and arrangements of color.

How did your recent collaboration with Coach come about? What was the experience like?
A creative director rang me out of the blue and then we talked on Skype. I loved this collaboration because they used my designs so inventively and brought them to the fashion world. It was thrilling to see my look floating down the runway (while sitting across from Anna Wintour). I loved their color choices. They took my bright palette and made it look like it was dipped in red wine, an idea that has influenced some of my projects since.

What was the last art show you saw that really moved you?
The work at the National Gallery of Victoria Triennial in Melbourne. Artist Yayoi Kusama invited visitors to cover every surface in an on-site "apartment" with artificial red gerbera daisies and stickers.

If you could host a dinner party for any artists dead or alive, who would you invite?
The artists Henri Matisse and Pierre Bonnard would be incredible to chat with about how they see the world, each so unique and both with an overactive sense of color that matches my own.

What were you thinking about when designing the solid-color and stranded stripes for MDK?
I was focused on making the stripes appealing to people new to working with lots of color.

And for those who are new to working with lots of color, what's your advice?
Start by following the directions in this Field Guide. The solid stripes are the perfect baby step toward working with more than one color at a time. The stranded stripes—made by repeating forms across the rows—are like music for the eyes. The color sequences are rhythmic so they are much easier to manage than they look.

ABBREVIATIONS

Approx: Approximately
Beg: Begin(ning)(s)
BO: Bind off
CO: Cast on
Dpn: Double-pointed needle(s)
K: Knit
P: Purl
Pm: Place marker
Rep: Repeat(ed)(ing)(s)
Rnd(s): Round(s)
RS: Right side
St st: Stockinette stitch (knit 1 row, purl 1 row when working flat; knit all rounds when working in the round)
St(s): Stitch(es)
Tog: Together
WS: Wrong side

COLORWAYS FOR SCARVES AND COWLS SHOWN

— **Graduated Stripes Mistake Rib Scarf, Dusty** (see page 14)
1 ball each Ginger, Delft, Tawny, Avocado, Seafarer, Amethyst, Peony, Scree

— **Graduated Stripes Tubular Scarf, Bright** (see page 5)
1 ball each Zinnia, Mineral, Vaseline Green, Barbara, Scree, Iris, Pink Bliss, Lotus Leaf

— **Coins Tubular Scarf, Two-Color** (see page 14)
3 balls each Seafarer and Clay

— **Checkerboard and Chevrons Tubular Scarf, Bright** (see page 18)
2 balls each Seafarer and Scree; 1 ball each Rage, Turquoise, Pink Bliss, Lotus Leaf, Electric Green, Tawny, Zinnia, Mineral, Frozen, Avocado, Amethyst, Barbara

— **Checkerboard and Chevrons Tubular Scarf, Dusty** (see page 18)
2 balls each Maritime and Alabaster; 1 ball each Pink Bliss, Peony, Camel, Clay, Avocado, Mineral, Amethyst, Frozen, Iris, Vaseline Green

— **Boxes Cowl, Dusty** (see page 39)
1 ball each Amethyst, Alabaster, Vaseline Green, Avocado, Pink Bliss, Maritime, Frozen, Zinnia, Iris

— **Coins Cowl, Dusty** (see page 39)
1 ball each Peony, Alabaster, Mineral, Pink Bliss, Amethyst, Scree, Avocado, Frozen, Vaseline Green